Recommended sticker(#1) and placement.

FRIENDSHIP

Friendship is a blessing that reaches heart to heart.

Recommended sticker (#2) and placement.

How blessings brighten as
they take their flight.

Edward Young

Recommended sticker (#3) and placement.

Add a touch of heaven
to your day—
Be thankful!

Add a touch of heaven
to your day—
Be thankful!

Recommended sticker (#4) and placement.

DAISY · ROSE · NARCISSUS · ORCHID · POPPY

HYDRANGEA

CYCLAMEN · TULIP · SUNFLOWER · VIOLET

The earth laughs
in flowers.
Ralph Waldo Emerson

Recommended sticker (#5) and placement.

Special times, forever to hold...
Memories with
friends are worth
more than gold.

Recommended sticker (#6) and placement.

Recommended sticker (#7) and placement.

Recommended sticker(#8) and placement.

HERBS

HOMEGROWN

Greenhouse

Family Farm

Give yourself
some time each
day to sit and
ponder, breathe,
and pray.

HERBS
HOMEGROWN
Greenhouse
Family Farm.

Give yourself
some time each
day to sit and
ponder, breathe,
and pray.

Recommended sticker (#9) and placement.

Recommended sticker (#10) and placement.

God shares His love
through the heart
of a friend.

God shares His love
through the heart
of a friend.

Recommended sticker (#11) and placement.

Recommended sticker (#12) and placement.

Every day brings a
chance to make a
beautiful difference
in the world.

Every day brings a
chance to make a
beautiful difference
in the world.

Recommended sticker (#13) and placement.

Stay positive!
Always expect something
good is on its way.

Recommended sticker (#14) and placement.

Recommended sticker (#15) and placement.

Sow the seeds of kindness...
and you will have
a harvest of blessings.

Sow the seeds of kindness...
and you will have
a harvest of blessings.

Recommended sticker (#16) and placement.

Simple joys
are the greatest gifts.

Simple joys
are the greatest gifts.

Recommended sticker (#17) and placement.

Coffee,
Conversation
& Friends
Always
Welcome

Recommended sticker (#18) and placement.

Count yourself blessed
every day and you will
find yourself living
in a world of blessings.

Recommended sticker (#19) and placement.

Family & Friends are life's greatest blessings.

Recommended sticker (#20) and placement.